Highlights™

PuzzleMania®
School Puzzles

HIGHLIGHTS PRESS
Honesdale, Pennsylvania

CONTENTS

When you finish a puzzle, check it off √.
Good luck, and happy puzzling!

Do the Math

Hidden Pictures®

Wordplay

Poetry Break

Brainteasers

Look Twice

A-Mazing!

Arts & Crafts

Catch This!

Thwack! It's a high-fly ball. Will it get over the fence? Follow the path of the ball to see if anyone can make the catch.

5

Funny Food

School lunch is no laughing matter—or is it? This lunchroom holds the answer to the riddle below. Read each clue to find out what letter goes in each numbered space. Hurry, before the bell rings for class.

1. This letter is on a lunch bag.
2. Look on a book bag for this letter.
3. You'll find this letter on a slice of pizza.
4. This letter is on a light.
5. This letter is being served.
6. Look for this letter on a hair band.
7. A janitor's got this letter.
8. You'll find this letter on a juice box.
9. Look on a window for this letter.
10. This letter is on a stack of trays.
11. Serve yourself this letter at the salad bar.

What do you call the rear of the lunchroom?

__ __ __   __ __ __ __ __ __ __ __
5 8 2   11 3 10 1 7 6 9 4

Hidden Pictures®
Froggie Freedom

drinking glass

lemon

lightning bolt

jug

elf's hat

hanger

slice of pie

wristwatch

bird

shark

closed book

fish

bowl

I Forgot My KROOMHEW

Mr. Clampett has heard plenty of excuses from kids who forgot to turn in their homework. He made a list of his favorite ones. Some of the words are scrambled. Unscramble them and see which excuse you think is the silliest.

A strange **ILENA** creature took it on his spaceship.

My baby **TERSIS** tore it up.

My **LIPNEC** broke.

The **HOLOCS** bus splashed mud on it.

A giant **DOONRAT** blew it away.

Here it is. I wrote it in **VINELBISI** ink.

A starving **TAC** ate it.

My mom was so proud she mailed it to my **NERMADGROTH**.

KROOMHEW? You didn't tell us we had KROOMHEW.

Illustrated by Mike Moran

9

Say Cheese!

Miss Noodleberg's class is getting ready for their school photo. Before the photographer finishes clicking, can you find at least **20** differences between these pictures?

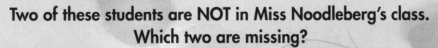

Illustrated by Genevieve Kote

DANCE MOVES

Fiona and three of her girlfriends are taking a ballroom dancing class. For the big recital, each girl is paired with one boy from the class and each couple performs one type of dance. From the clues below, can you figure out the pairs and their dances?

Use the chart to keep track of your answers. Put an **X** in each box that can't be true and an **O** in boxes that match.

	Sammy	Luke	Owen	Will	Fox-trot	Jitterbug	Tango	Cha-cha-cha
Fiona					X	X	O	X
Ashley					X	X	X	O
Sofia							X	X
Caryn					X	O	X	X

1. Fiona never tries any type of dance with more than two syllables in its name.

2. Owen and Ashley hit it off as partners and agreed not to do any dance with an animal in its name.

3. The two kids with the same first initial danced the fox-trot.

4. Luke never tries any dance with fewer than three syllables in its name.

By the Numbers

Meet the Dakota Dunkers. The five starters wear numbers that add to exactly 100. That leaves one super sub to come in off the bench. Can you figure out which player is the super sub? (Hint: Try adding up all the numbers and then see if you can figure it out!)

THE Run DOWN

It's time for the big All-State Cross-Country Race. Follow each runner to see what place she comes in. On your mark, get set, go!

Illustrated by Daryll Collins

15

TRY 10

1. Circle the object that does not rhyme with fun.

2. A "baker's dozen" is how ma[...]
○ 11   ○ 13   ○ 24

3. Can you think of four hair colors?

4. If someone is "under the weather," he or she isn't feeling well.
○ True   ○ False

5. Name thre[...] things you migh[...] at the beach.

. "Camisa" is Spanish for what
ece of clothing?
pants   ○ hat   ○ shirt

7. Circle the plate with more
acorns on it.

8. Name two sports
where you kick a ball.

. New Mexico touches the
cific Ocean.
True   ○ False

10. Can you think of five words
that can be made using some of the
letters in AIRPLANE?

AIRPLANE

Illustrated by Kelly Kennedy

17

Abraham Lincoln

By Aileen Fisher

His lot was hard
and his future bleak—
Abraham Lincoln
of Pigeon Creek.

He studied law
though a backwoods boy—
Abraham Lincoln
of Illinois.

In politics
he somehow won—
Abraham Lincoln
of Washington.

Rarely a man
more loved than he—
Abraham Lincoln
of history!

Back to the Drawing Board

Are you feeling crafty? We've gathered 16 arts and crafts supplies for you. Their names fit into the grid in just one way. Use the number of letters in each word as a clue to where it might fit.

4 Letters
CLAY
FELT
GLUE
YARN

5 Letters
BEADS
PAPER
RULER

6 Letters
CANVAS
ERASER
PAINTS

7 Letters
BRUSHES
~~CRAYONS~~
GLITTER
MARKERS
PASTELS

8 Letters
SCISSORS

CRAYONS

Zoo Q's

Feed Me!

Can you help the zookeeper get dinner to the lions on time?

Start

Finish

JUMBLED ANIMALS

Unscramble each set of letters to get the name of a zoo animal.

BRAZE — — — — —

MELAC — — — — —

ADNAP — — — — —

TEACHHE — — — — — — —

RAPLO RABE — — — — — — — — — —

GUESS WHO?

Can you figure out what these three animals are?

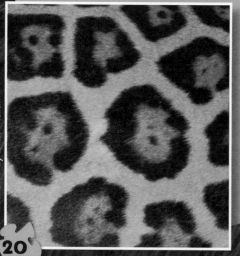

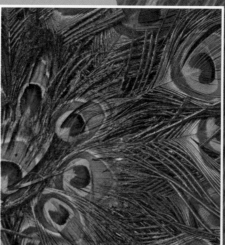

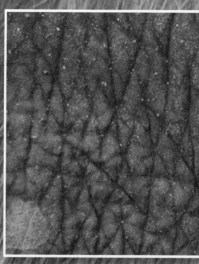

Land or Sea?

Do you know which of these animals live on the land and which live in the water?

KOMODO DRAGON
BRITTLESTAR
ALPACA
MANATEE
STINGRAY
CHINCHILLA
BONGO
BARRACUDA

Balancing Act

The zookeeper found this seal balancing something amazing on its nose! Draw in what you think it is.

Missing Vowels

PRMT is the word *primate* with the vowels taken away. Can you figure out the name of these five prmts?

_____
CHMPNZ

_____
BBN

_____
GRLL

_____
SPDR MNKY

_____
RNGTN

bird

sock

hammer

snail

sailboat

baseball bat

banana

candle

golf club

football

slice of pizza

hockey stick

Dot to Dot

Connect the dots from 1 to 27 to see what the winner gets.

1ST

Illustration by Dave Klug

23

What's Bugging You?

When Molly sat down in the cafeteria, there was a **spider on the table**! Lots of people had something to say about it. Unscramble each word in capital letters to see what each person told her.

1. The **cafeteria worker** asked, "Would it like a burger and SEFLI?"
   F L I E S

2. The **English teacher** said, "May I have a DROW with it?"
   — — — —

3. The **principal** said, "No STEP allowed at school!"
   — — — —

4. The **secretary** said, "I've never seen this YPET before."
   — — — —

5. The **monitor** said, "No creeping down the LAHL!"
   — — — —

6. The **school bus driver** said, "Don't let it go for a NIPS."
   — — — —

7. The **swim coach** said, "Let's see if it can do the WALCR."
   — — — — —

8. The **computer teacher** said, "I'll see if it has its own BEW TIES."
   — — — —   — — — —

9. The **music teacher** said, "Don't let the itsy bitsy critter go up the TROUTWASPE."
   — — — — — — — — — —

10. The **math teacher** said, "Catch it quick, before it PLUMTILSIES!"
    — — — — — — — — — — —

24

Heading Home

It's the first day of the new school year. Max and his friends each have a different homeroom. Using the clues below, can you figure out which teacher and homeroom number each friend has?

Use the chart to keep track of your answers. Put an **X** in each box that can't be true and an **O** in boxes that match.

	Ms. Russell	Mr. Jones	Ms. Wilson	Mr. Tripp	Ms. Ames	25	50	Rooms 100	125	200
Max										
Robert										
Jessica										
Willow										
Mia										

1. The number of Willow's room, with Mr. Tripp, is five times as big as the number of Max's room.

2. One friend's name ends in the same letter that his or her teacher's name begins with.

3. Mia's room number is half that of Jessica's.

4. One friend's name shares the same set of double letters as his or her teacher's name.

5. Robert is in Ms. Wilson's room, which has the highest number.

Swim Meet

Kiera wants to meet her friend at the far end of the pool.
Can you find the one path that will take her there?

Start

B

I J

N

S

T

C

A

S

E

R

A

Q

BONUS PUZZLE

Did you find the path? Now write all the letters you found on it, in order, in the spaces below. They'll answer the riddle.

Where do minivans go swimming?

___ ___ ___   ___ ___ ___ ___ ___ ___

Illustrated by Ron Zalme

5, 4, 3, 2, 1...

Inside this rocket are **34** space terms. Your mission is to boldly go up, down, across, backwards, and diagonally. Circle all the words that you find. When you are finished, write the leftover letters in order in the spaces below the rocket. They will give you an important message from mission control.

Word List

ARMS	RE-ENTRY
CARGO	BOOSTERS
FORCE	FAIL-SAFE
MOONS	MOMENTUM
ORBIT	MOUNTAIN
SALVO	NOSE CONE
~~APOGEE~~	THRUSTER
ATOMIC	CELESTIAL
COSMOS	ASTRONAUTS
FUNDED	SPLASHDOWN
LANDER	SPACE DEBRIS
RAMJET	CAPE CANAVERAL
RANGER	GUIDANCE SYSTEMS
CAPSULES	MANNED SPACESHIP
CONTROL	ZOOM
MISSION	ZERO
PERIGEE	
NECK-WRENCHING G-FORCES	

28

Word search puzzle (rocket-shaped grid):

```
            S
        A   I   O
        P   R   S
        E   B   M
    Z   R   E   E   S
    P   I   D   T   S
    I   G   E   Y   S   E
    H   E   C   Y   S   C
    S   E   A   S   R   R
    E   E   P   E   O   F
    C   L   S   C   O   G
    R   A   A   U   N   G   T
O   S   P   N   L   A   G   B   I
F   H   S   S   D   E   D   N   U   F   B
Z   D   N   L   D   E   S   I   I   O   A   A   R
B O O S T E R S   U   H   A   I   S   E   O
W O R E G N A R G   C   S   L   S   T   L
N M M O U N T A I N T   S   A   S   A   M
R C A P E C A N A V E R A   L   U   I   O
E O A A T O M I C J R O F V   R   T   M
E N O C E S O N M T W N E O   H   S   E
N T O   M G A   F K A   T   E   N
R R O   O R C   U   L   E   U
Y L F   A C S   N   C   M
```

Mission control says, " _ _ _ _ _ _   _ _ _ !"

29

Illustrated by Garry Colby

Crafts

Back-to-School Bus Frame

By April Theis

1. Cut two identical bus shapes from **poster board**. Carefully cut windows in one of them.
2. With a parent's permission, tape a **photo** behind each window. Glue the bus shapes together.
3. Draw details on the bus with a **marker**. Cut a stop sign from **colored paper** and glue it.
4. For wheels, cover four clean **applesauce cups** with **masking tape**. Paint them with black **acrylic paint**. Cover the openings of the cups with **craft-foam** circles.
5. Glue the wheels to the bottom of the bus to make the frame stand up.

Study Buddy Doorknob Hanger

By Olive Howie

1. Draw an owl on **thin cardboard**. Cut it out. For a hanger, glue a loop of **yarn** to the top of the shape.
2. Glue **colored paper** onto both sides of the cardboard. Cut features from paper and glue them on. Add details with **markers**.
3. Write *GUESS WHOOO IS STUDYING?* on one side. Leave the other side blank. Hang the study buddy on your doorknob. Flip it to show when you are studying.

Book Boxes

By Anne Bell

1. Cut the tops off several empty **boxes**. Cover them with **colored paper**. Use **markers** to write book titles on the boxes.
2. Glue the "books" together at the sides. Trace the bottom onto a piece of **thin cardboard**. Cut out the shape and glue it to the bottom of the books.
3. Store pencils, markers, and other school supplies in the book boxes.

Photos by Hank Schneider, except page 31 (top) by Guy Cali Associates, Inc. and photos in bus frame by Thinkstock.

Personalized Bag Tag

By Christina Hackney

1. Cut a shape from **thin cardboard**. Punch a hole near the top.
2. Trace the shape twice onto **craft foam**. Cut out the pieces and punch matching holes.
3. Glue a foam shape to each side of the cardboard shape.
4. Write your name on both sides with a **marker**, **glitter glue**, or **puffy paint**.
5. Loop a **rubber band** through the hole. Loop the other end through a strap on a backpack.

Alphabet Game

By Kristin Baldwin

Draw a trail with 26 squares on white **poster board**. Write the letters of the alphabet on it. Cut out the trail and glue it to colored poster board. Cut a home and school from **colored paper**. Add details with cut paper and **markers**. Glue them to the game board. Add **stickers**.

To make a spinner, draw four equal parts on a **plastic lid**. Label them *1, 2, 3,* and *4.* Poke a hole through the center of the lid. Push a **brass fastener** through a **paper clip** and the top of the spinner. Bend the fastener ends and tape them down. Make a second spinner labeled *Foods, Books, Animals,* and *Places.* Glue both spinners to the game board. To make a "book" game piece, cut three small rectangles from white **craft foam**. Glue them in a stack. Cut a "book cover" from colored craft foam. Glue it around the stack. Place a real book on top while it dries. Make one game piece for each player.

To Play: Start from home. Spin the number spinner. Move that number of spaces, then spin the category spinner. Name a word in that category that starts with the letter on which you landed. If you can't think of a word, move back a space and try that letter instead.

Players take turns. When a player reaches the school, he or she must name a word in each category that starts with the first letter of his or her first or last name. The first person to reach the school and provide all four words wins!

Hidden Pictures®
Making a Mural

hatchet

spool of thread

teacup

bowl

sailboat

slipper

sock

spoon

pencil

toothbrush

coffeepot

banana

Tic Tac Row

Each of these planets has something in common with the other two planets in the same row. For example, in the top row across each planet has red spots. Look at the other rows across, down, and diagonally. Can you tell what's alike in each row?

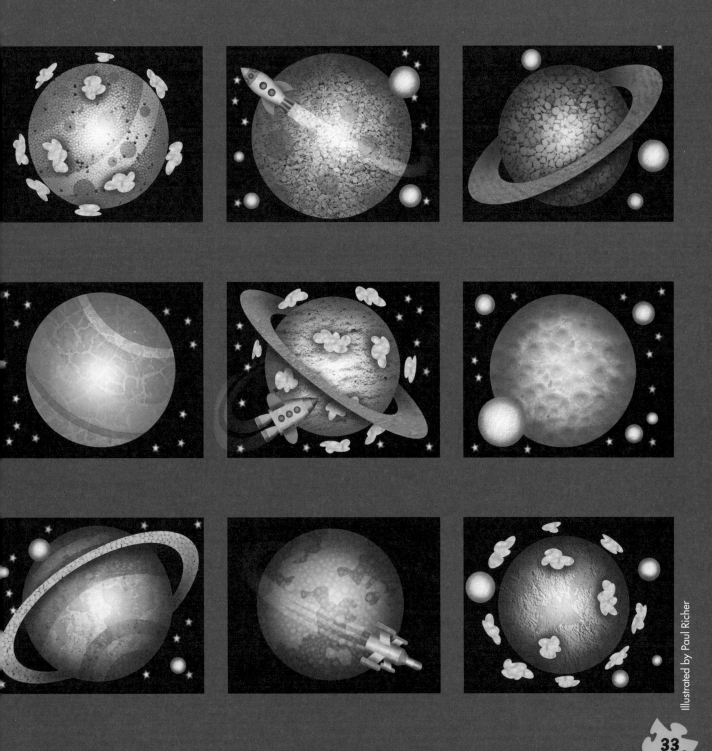

Illustrated by Paul Richer

THiS Page Has Been Bugged

Each beetle has one that matches it exactly.
Can you find each matching pair?

Illustrated by Wendy Wax

Jungle Journey

This scientist has gotten lost in the rain forest. Can you help her find the way back to her canoe?

Start

Finish

TWiN TOUCANS

Which two toucan pictures are exactly alike?

A

B

C

D

Rain Forest Quiz Match each question to the right answer.

1. Continent with the most rain forest land
2. World's largest rain forest river
3. Zebra-like rain forest animal
4. Rain forest butterfly
5. Continent that's home to the Congo Rain Forest

a. Okapi
b. Africa
c. Blue Morpho
d. Amazon
e. South America

Creature or Not?

Some of these are rain forest creatures and some are imposters. Can you tell which are the real critters?

CHIMICHANGA or CHIMPANZEE?
GIBBON or RIBBON?
FEMUR or LEMUR?
PIRANHA or KIELBASA?
ANACONDA or EMPANADA?
STAMEN or CAIMAN?

Missing Vowels

NMLS is the word *animals* with the vowels taken away. Can you identify each of these tropical rain forest animals?

SPDR MNKY

TR FRG

GRLL

JGR

RNGTN

New Species

More than half of the world's plant and animal species live in the rain forest. Scientists estimate that millions of rain forest species are still undiscovered. What new living thing would you like to find? Draw it here.

What's It Worth?

A=   B=   C=   D=   E=   F=

1. $E + B = D$

2. $B + F = C$

3.
$$\begin{array}{r} E \\ \times\, F \\ \hline F \end{array}$$

4.
$$\begin{array}{r} A \\ A \\ A \\ A \\ +\, A \\ \hline BA \end{array}$$

5.
$$\begin{array}{r} C \\ C \\ C \\ C \\ +\, C \\ \hline DC \end{array}$$

Illustrated by John Nez

38

Double Cross

Can you shed some light on this puzzle? To find the answer to the riddle below, first cross out all the pairs of matching letters. Then write the remaining letters in order in the spaces beneath the riddle.

SS	BB	LL	IM	QQ	CC	TT
VE	DD	XX	EE	OO	RY	JJ
NN	WW	II	PL	ZZ	AA	KK
UU	EA	SS	LL	HH	OO	SE
RR	DD	DT	VV	EE	II	MM
YY	UU	OO	OH	PP	CC	EA
GG	TT	TY	AA	KK	OU	EE

What did the sun say when it was introduced to Earth?

_'_ ____ ___

__ ___ ____

___ ___.

Basketball Bloopers

There are some strange sights at this basketball game. Can you find at least **25** odd, weird, or wacky things in this picture?

TRY 10

1. Name three things you eat with a spoon.

2. Which has the fewest sides?
○ square   ○ triangle   ○ rectan

3. Circle the item that does not rhyme with luck.

4. Name two oceans.

5. Seattle, Washington, is known as the "Big Apple."
○ True   ○ False

. The Spanish word "sol"
eans what?

○ salt   ○ space   ○ sun

7. Name two instruments
with strings.

8. Name three
things that are worn
around the neck.

. St. Patrick's
ay is in March.

○ True   ○ False

10. Circle the monkey with
more bananas.

Illustrated by Kelly Kennedy

43

DRINK SEARCH

There are lots of drink containers at the sch

PLEASE RECYCLE

DRINK MORE
MILK

TRASH

Can you find?

- 1 squirrel
- 2 oranges
- 3 sandwiches
- 4 backpacks

Illustrated by Scott Burroughs

45

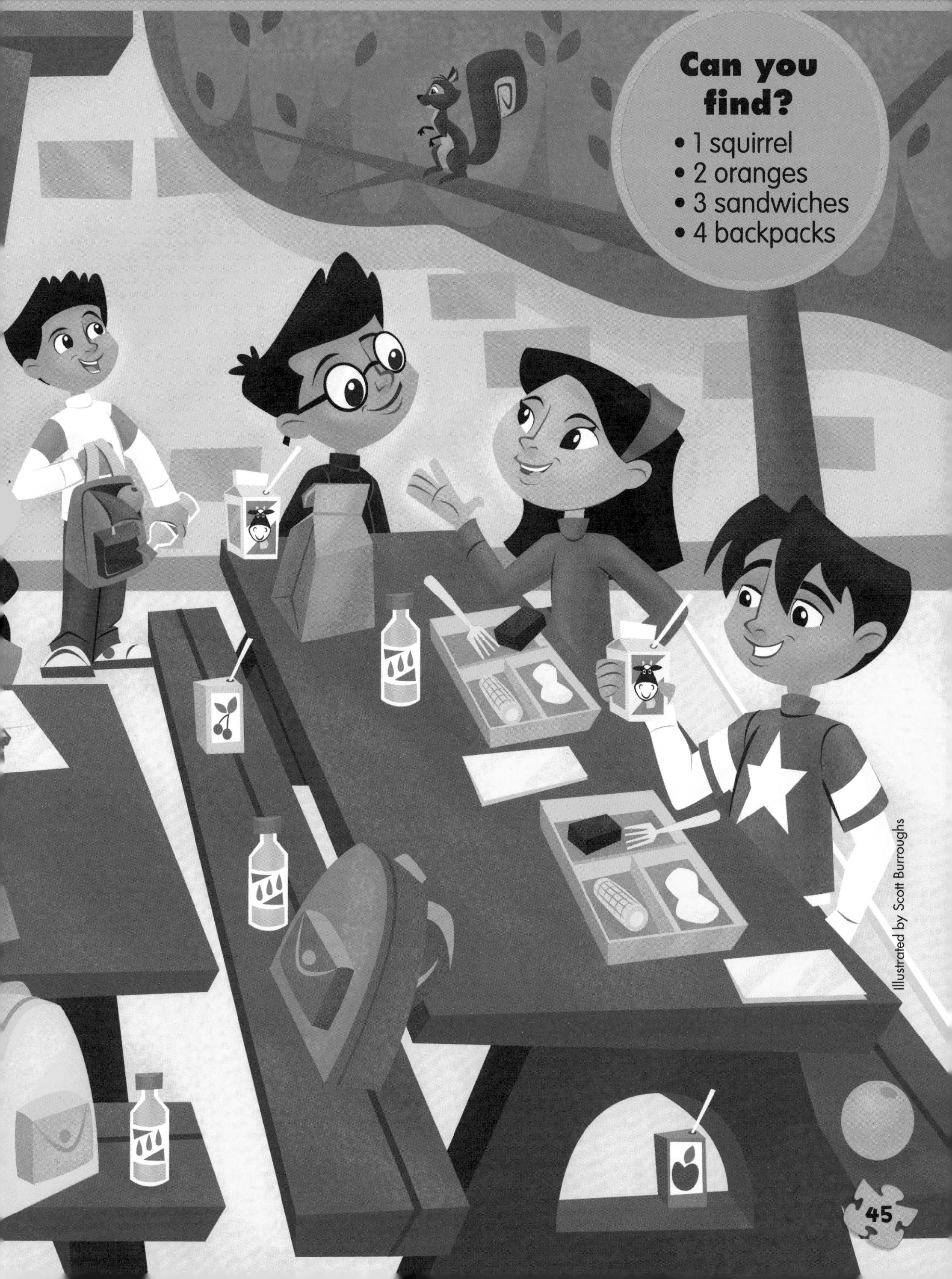

Be Seated

Mr. Ease has six boys and six girls in his class: Aiden, Brian, Carlos, Dave, Eric, and Frank; Grace, Haley, Iris, Jada, Katie, and Lily. But who sits where? Use the clues below to figure out which seat belongs to which kid. The numbers on the chairs will help.

1. Dave sits in the seat farthest from the clock.

2. Brian sits between Lily and Katie and behind Haley.

3. Eric sits between Haley and Jada, behind Iris, and in front of Lily.

4. The girls all sit in even-numbered seats, the boys in odd-numbered seats.

5. Grace, Carlos, and Katie sit in the rows farthest away from the windows.

6. Jada sits behind Frank and in front of Dave.

1 _____

2 _____

3 _____

4 _____

8 _____

7 _____

6 _____

5 _____

9 Dave

10 _____

11 _____

12 _____

Hidden Pictures®
School Shopping

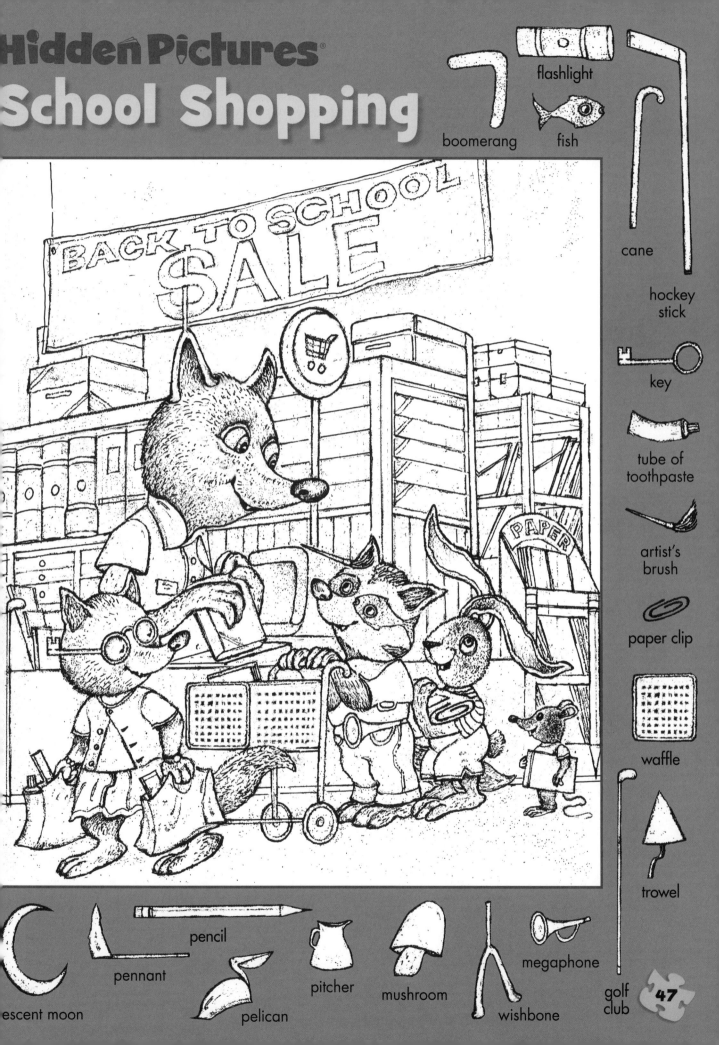

boomerang

flashlight

fish

cane

hockey stick

key

tube of toothpaste

artist's brush

paper clip

waffle

trowel

crescent moon

pennant

pencil

pelican

pitcher

mushroom

wishbone

megaphone

golf club

Go Team!

Get ready to tackle a fun puzzle. In this crossword, every answer is made up of letters from the phrase

GAME-WINNING TOUCHDOWN.

We kicked in the first one for you. Can you score the rest of the answers?

Across

1 Zilch, nada, zip
8 It could be full or crescent-shaped.
9 12:00 a.m.
11 Where a pet bird might live
12 Opposite of bad
14 Mexican fast food
17 Twelve hours after 9 Across
18 What a dog does with its tail
19 A nickel or a dime
21 Opposite of guilty
23 One-twelfth of a foot
24 It might be snow-capped.
26 Not nice
27 A cat noise

Down

2 An owl's call
3 Jewel
4 Move to music
5 It helps a door open and shut.
6 Beijing is its capital.
7 Curtains might hang around this.
10 Popular baseball park food
13 Atlantic or Pacific
15 5… 4… 3… 2… 1…
16 A veggie that makes you cry
18 How heavy you are
20 The color of snow
22 A narrow boat with paddles
24 Long horse hair
25 "_____, you're it!"

NOTHING

49

Color Q's

Oops!

Hugh has painted himself into a corner. Can you help him find a path out?

Finish

Start

Illustrated by Mike Moran

RED

Color Definitions

See if you can guess whether or not each of these color expressions is true or false.

- If a company is **in the red**, it means it made lots of money.

- Someone who is **green with envy** is hardly jealous at all.

- If you are **tickled pink**, you are extremely happy.

- A **yellow-bellied** person is very brave.

- If something happens **once in a blue moon**, it almost never happens.

Shady Quiz

Each group of three words describes shades of a color. Use your color I.Q. to figure out which ones.

Crimson	Ruby	Scarlet	_____
Azure	Cobalt	Teal	_____
Sage	Chartreuse	Jade	_____
Plum	Mauve	Lavender	_____
Amber	Citron	Canary	_____

A CUP-PLE OF COLORS?

Only two stacks of paint cups are the same. Can you find the matching stacks?

Your Masterpiece

Can you turn these splotches of paint into a work of art?

AN ANIMAL OF ANOTHER COLOR?

The colors in the names of these animals have been mixed up.
Can you move the colors around to fix them?

Great Yellow Shark _____

Brown Jay _____

White Widow Spider _____

Blue-Eyed Tree Frog _____

Black Jacket _____

Red Bear _____

51

There is more than meets the eye on this school field trip.
Can you find the hidden objects?

Illustrated by Dave Klug

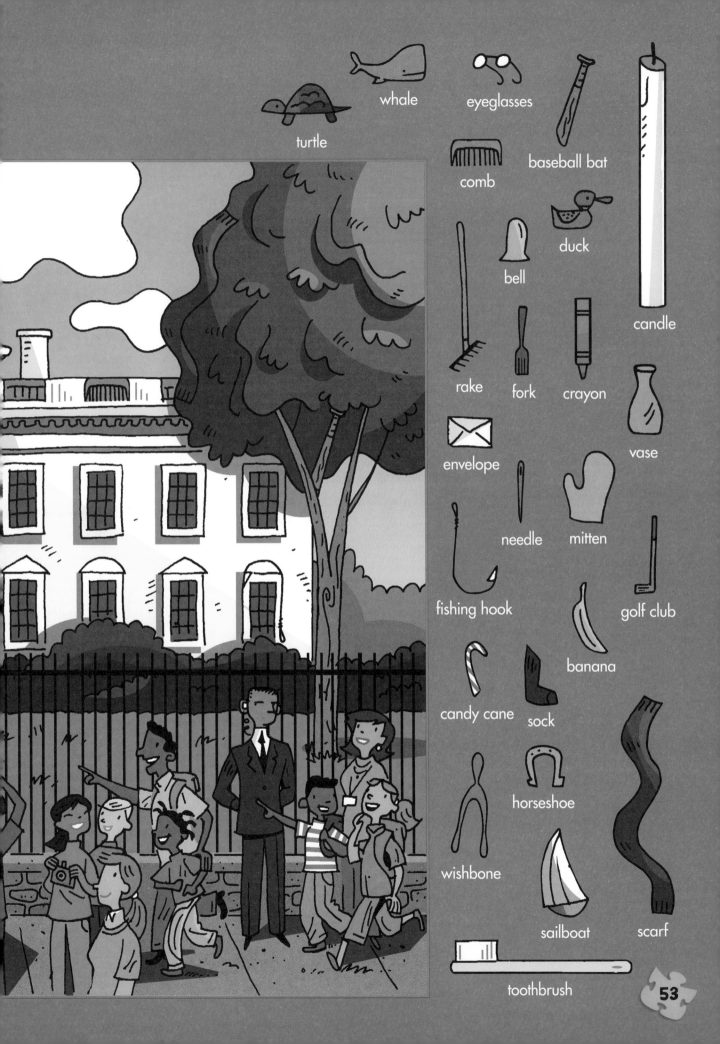

turtle

whale

eyeglasses

comb

baseball bat

duck

bell

candle

rake

fork

crayon

vase

envelope

needle

mitten

fishing hook

banana

golf club

candy cane

sock

horseshoe

wishbone

sailboat

scarf

toothbrush

An Apple a Day

Open wide! This puzzle is filled with **17** mouth-watering kinds of apples. They are hidden up, down, across, backwards, and diagonally. When you've found them all, look for four wiggling **WORM**s hiding in the apple.

Word List

- ~~BALDWIN~~
- BRAEBURN
- CORTLAND
- CRISPIN
- DELICIOUS
- EMPIRE
- FUJI
- GALA
- GRANNY SMITH
- IDARED
- JONATHAN
- MCINTOSH
- MUTSU
- PAULA RED
- PIPPIN
- ROME
- WINESAP

```
        R M W
        M I   M R O W R
        N R U B E A R B
        E   M W O R M
        S
    U W W R   A   N O W M
    O F S N I P P I P W G W W
  J R W U T W W P A U L A R E D
  W O G T J U S (N I W D L A B) R
  W R N H T I M S Y N N A R G W
  G I D A R E D E L I C I O U S
  W W C T H S O T N I C M M
    O O O H W E R I P M E
    R D N A L T R O C
    M M W N M R O W
```

54

Tic Tac Row

Each of these robots has something in common with the other two robots in the same row. For example, in the first row across all three robots are on wheels. Look at the other rows across, down, and diagonally. Can you tell what's alike in each row?

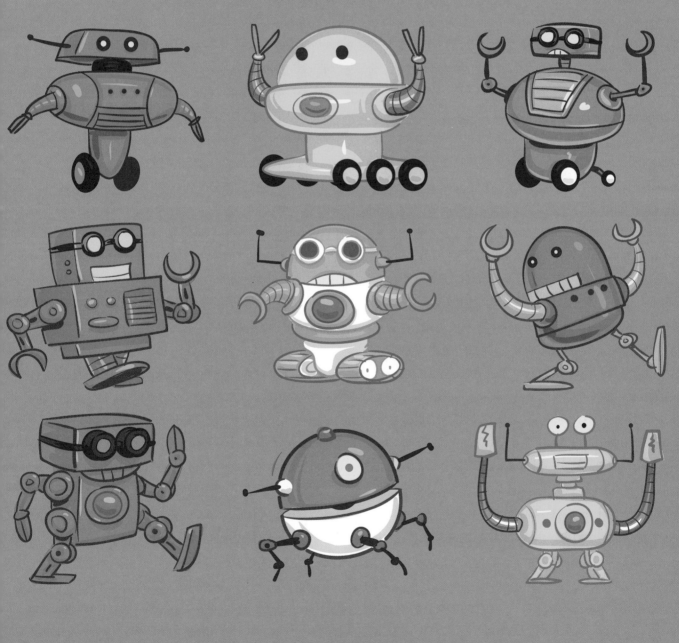

Lab Labyrinth

Dr. Zarkoff has finally completed his Fliddersplidgit. But will it work? To test his invention, the world-famous scientist is dropping a jelly bean into the beaker. Will it make it to his faithful assistant Igor? Find a path that leads from **START** to **FINISH**.

Start

Finish

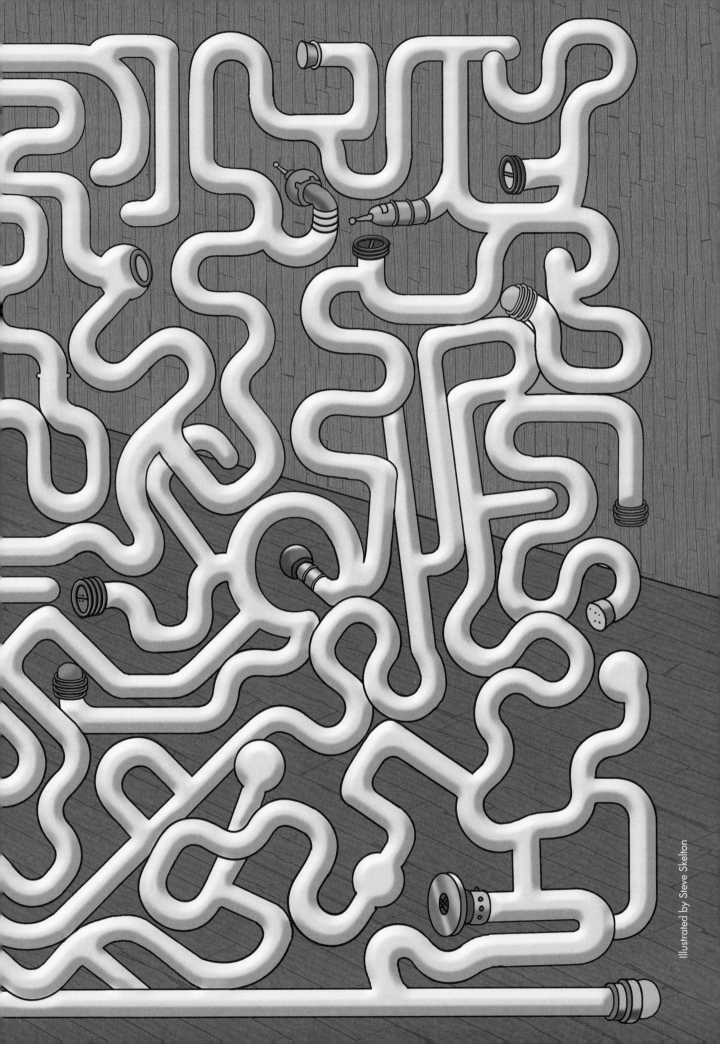

Illustrated by Steve Skelton

TRY 10

1. Circle the picture that does not rhyme with roast.

2. Can you think of four states with two words in their names?

3. Name four animals that start with the letter S.

4. How many quarts are in two gallons?

○ 4   ○ 6   ○ 8

5. The word "pastel" is Spanish for cake.

○ True   ○ False

6. A car that runs on gas and ectricity is called what?
- a hybrid
- a hyphen
- a hyena

7. Benjamin Franklin was a U.S. president.
○ True   ○ False

8. Can you name three words that have an OO in them?

9. Circle the unk with more ickers.

10. Name four foods you eat cold.

Illustrated by Kelly Kennedy

59

nail

ring

hammer

fork

golf club

mallet

comb

leaf

canoe

banana

eyeglasses

toothbrush

spoon

lollipop

60

GOOFY GYMNASIUM

How many silly things can you find in this picture?

CRAYON SEARCH

There are crayons all over this classroom.

Crafts

Bookmark Buddies

Make these book pals to help you keep your place.

1. Paint the craft stick or tongue depressor. Let dry, then decorate with markers or paint.

2. Bend a 2-inch piece of chenille stick in half to form a V. Glue the V to one end of the craft stick, pointing up.

3. Glue on a pompon head and plastic wiggle eyes. Let dry.

More Ideas

Decorate a potted houseplant with a craft-stick worm poking out of the dirt.

If your pompon head is large enough, you can glue the chenille-stick V to the pompon.

QUICK REACTION

It's simply my reaction
Who cares
what it's abo...
I reach for sat...
with my tongue...
I stick it out.

NOT FORGOT

I forgot to take the trash out;
    you didn't tell me that's my job.
I forgot to bring my money;
    you never know when you'll get robbed.
I forgot that game ar...

The Joys of Snowboarding

I laugh out loud
As I float through powder,
Float through the fluffy snow.

I do a front flip
And laugh even louder.
Big air—the way to go!

Down to the lift
Then up again,
Making this board behave

As I speed down the hill
In graceful arcs,
Surfing the winter wave.

The Snowboarder

Snow, soft, white
In the morning light
Takeoff! And I'm in flight.

Down the hill
In the vivid chill
Bumps, jumps, and nary a spill.

Never knew I could

Ribbon-Weave Trivet

In and out, slow and steady, and you'll create this "hot" gift for your favorite cook.

You Will Need:
- thirteen craft sticks
- fabric ribbon

1. Glue four sticks together to form a square frame.
2. Glue nine sticks side by side, on top of the square frame. Leave a small space between each stick. Let dry.
3. Cut several pieces of ribbon about 10 inches long.
4. Weave the first ribbon in and out of the sticks. Leave at least 2 inches of ribbon dangling on each side of the square. Weave the second ribbon next to the first, using the opposite pattern. If you went under the first slat with the first ribbon, go OVER the first slat with the second ribbon. Repeat until the trivet is covered.
5. Glue the loose ends of the ribbons underneath the trivet.

More Ideas
Use different widths of ribbon to create different designs.

A Memento for Teacher

Tell your favorite teacher you care.

You Will Need:
- four craft sticks
- stiff black felt
- white gel pen or fabric paint
- red and green construction paper
- ribbon or yarn

1. Glue four craft sticks together to make a square.
2. Cut a square of black felt a bit smaller than the craft-stick square.
3. Write your message on the felt with a white gel pen or white fabric paint. Let dry. Glue the felt square to the back of the craft-stick square.
4. Cut four apple shapes from red construction paper, and glue to each corner of the frame. Add green leaves.
5. Glue a ribbon hanger to the back.

More Ideas
Write your message on paper before you write it on the felt, so you know exactly what you want to say and how you want to write it.

Cut out baseballs or footballs, glue them to the frame, and give it to your dad or grandfather on Father's Day.

Space Q's

Planet X?

Can you name the planet shown in each photo?

Space Out!

Outer space is home to solar systems, stars, and satellites. It also contains lots of words. Can you make at least 20 words from the letters of OUTER SPACE?

_____   _____

_____   _____

_____   _____

_____   _____

_____   _____

_____   _____

_____   _____

_____   _____

Moon Walk

Can you help this astronaut get back to his ship?

START

FINISH

Illustrated by Mike Dammer

Look-Alike Landers

Which two robotic landers are the same?

Welcome to Gluumgus

The sun never shines on Planet Gluumgus and the rain falls sideways. Draw a picture of an alien who would like living on Gluumgus.

Hey, I can see my house!

Space Dates

Match each of these events to the year it happened.

First man on the moon ●   ● 1976

First man in space ●   ● 1965

First space walk ●   ● 1969

First spacecraft landing on Mars ●   ● 1961

Bagel Bakers

The cooking class has been baki[ng]
bagels. Can you tell how ma[ny]
bagels each person baked as w[ell]
as how many bagels were bak[ed]
altogether? Hint: Start by figuring o[ut]
how many bagels Larry bake[d]

Andre baked half as many as Chuck.

Betty baked as many bagels as both Jane and Larry together.

Chuck baked twice as many as Larry.

Donna baked half as many as Glenn.

Glenn baked 10 more bagels than Betty.

Jane baked 4 more bagels than Andre.

Larry baked $3\frac{1}{2}$ dozen bagels.

Mary baked 7 more bagels than Donna.

Pablo baked half as many bagels as Sue.

Sue baked half as many bagels as Mary.

Illustrated by John Nez

SQUARE Off!

Can you figure out what animal appears in each picture?
Unscramble the name of each.

ASNEK

DRIZAL

LETTUR

GORILLATA

What do they all have in common?

All Aboard!

School's out! Time to get on the bus and head home. Before everyone climbs on, see if you can find at least **20** differences between these pictures.

Use these clues to figure out which kid on this page is JJ:

- JJ has a backpack.
- JJ has a blue shirt.
- JJ does not have a ponytail.

an you find these 12 items hidden in this lighthouse scene?

shoe

birthday cake

saucepan

turtle

eyeglasses

rhinoceros

scarf

comb

kite

magnifying glass

banana

arrow

Illustration by Dave Klug

Dot to Dot

Connect the dots from 1 to 22 to see
someone who likes lighthouses.

On the Wrong Track

There are some strange sights at the track meet today. Can you find at least **25** odd, weird, or wacky things in this picture? Ready, set, go!

¡GO!

MAIN ST.

75

Tic Tac Row

Each of these frogs has something in common with the other two frogs in the same row. For example, in the first row across all three frogs have stripes. Look at the other rows across, down, and diagonally. Can you tell what's alike in each row?

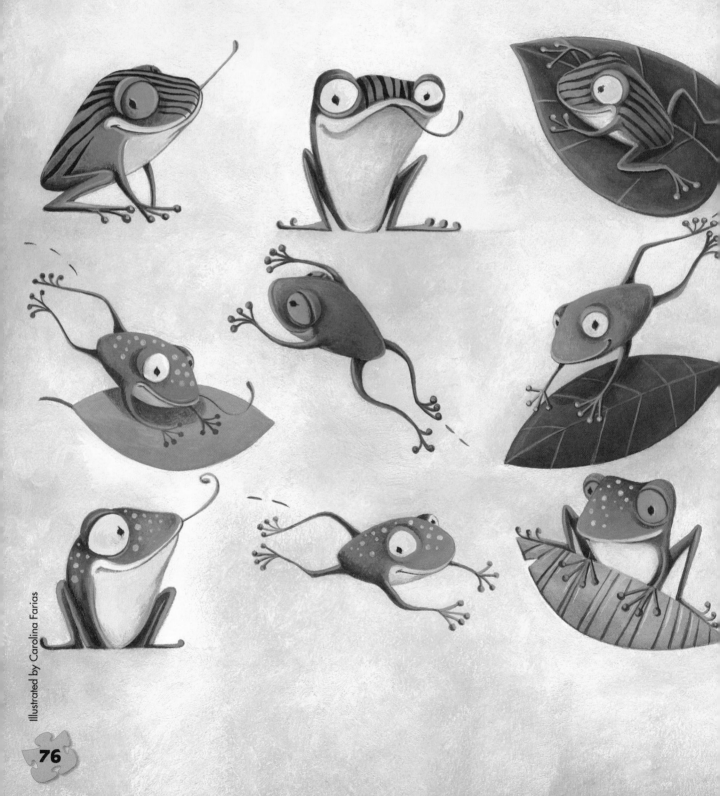

Hidden Pictures®
Practice Makes Perfect

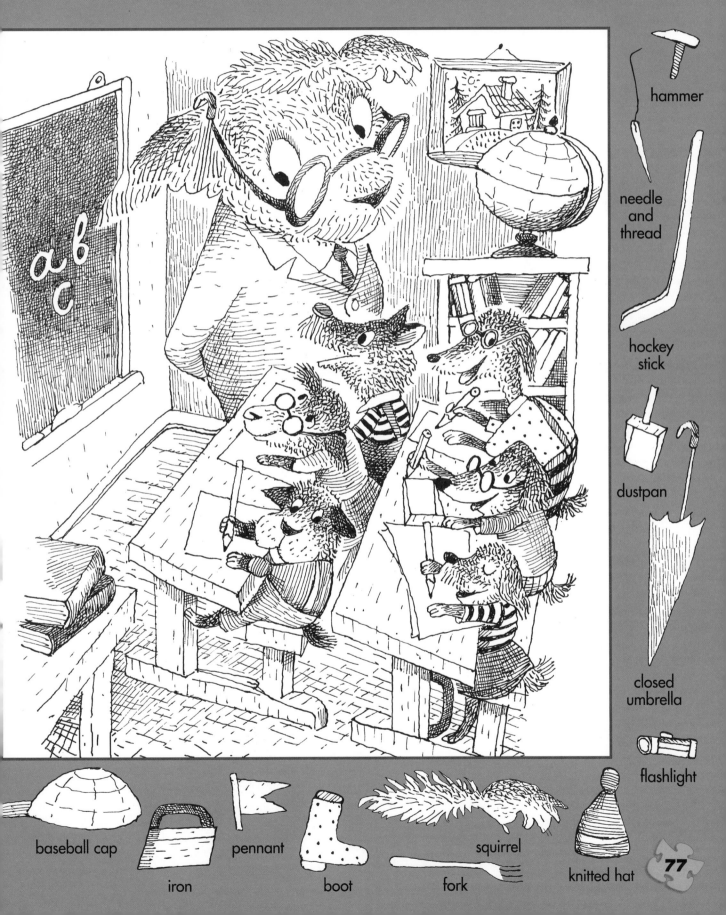

hammer

needle and thread

hockey stick

dustpan

closed umbrella

flashlight

baseball cap

iron

pennant

boot

fork

squirrel

knitted hat

JUMP ON It!

These jump ropers need to find their partners. Follow each rope to see who is partnered with whom. Go ahead, jump on in!

79

Note Worthy

Reed found a secret note tucked in his desk during music class. Can you help him read it? To crack the code, first write down each letter that has a number 1 above it in order in the spaces below. Then do the same with number 2 letters, then number 3, and so on, until you've filled in all the blanks.

```
3   5   2   7   1   4   1   8   2
B   S   S   H   D   B   E   Y   E

3   9   4   5   6   1   1   3   7
A   M   R   O   R   A   R   N   I

6   8   7   4   1   7   9   2   6
E   O   G   I   R   H   E   E   A

7   1   4   5   2   3   6   1   8
N   E   N   Y   Y   D   C   E   U

3   4   5   2   3   6   4   8   1
P   G   O   O   R   H   A   R   D

5   4   9   7   2   6   4   9   8
U   L   L   O   U   T   A   O   F

3   8   7   3   2   6   8   5   4
A   R   T   C   A   H   I   C   D

3   4   7   8   5   9   3   2   3
T   D   E   E   A   D   I   T   C

4   8   9   5   6   3   7   4   8
E   N   Y   N   E   E   S   R   D
```

D E A R _ _ _ _ _ ,

_ _ _ _ _ _ _ _ _ _ _ _ _ _ .

_ _ _ _ _ _ _ _ _ _ _ _ _ _ _ _ _

_ _ _ _ _ _ _ _ _ _ _ _ _ _ _ _ _ ! ☺

_ _ _ _ _ _ _ _ _ _ _ ,

_ _ _ _ _

80

Silly Schoolyard

How many silly things can you find in this picture?

Illustrated by Karen Stormer

TRY 10

1. Circle the object that does not rhyme with locket.

2. Tumble, vault, and balance beam are all words from what sp
- gymnastics
- swimming
- volleyball

3. Name three things you might put in a shake or a smoothie.

4. Name two states that start with the letter I.

I ← 10 MILES

5. A nickel is bigger in size than a quarter.
- True
- False

6. The word "rojo" is Spanish for hich color?

○ purple ○ red ○ pink

7. Name three sounds you might hear at a circus.

8. Circle the ball you would serve.

9. Linguine, bows, and rotini e all types of hat?

10. Teddy bears were named for U.S. president Teddy Roosevelt.
○ True ○ False

PENCIL SEARCH

Grab a pencil and start looking.

$4 + 8 = 12$

MATH

ENGLISH

Can you find?

- 1 mouse
- 2 smiley faces
- 3 ponytails
- 4 crayons

Illustrated by Scott Burroughs

Get Coordinated

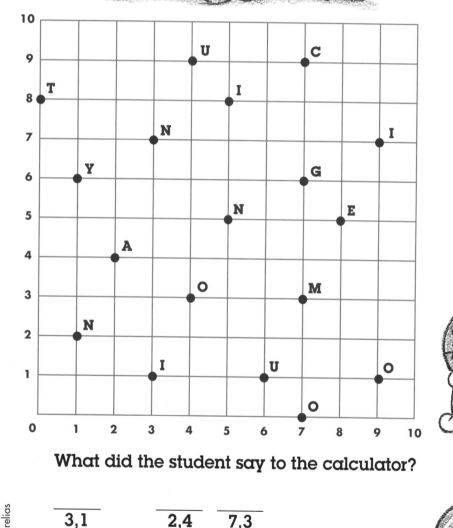

To answer this riddle, you'll need to find the right letter on the grid that matches the pair of numbers under each blank space. That pair of numbers is the "coordinate"— the place on the grid where the number from the horizontal line and the number on the vertical line meet. The first number in each pair tells you how many lines to count across the bottom. The second number tells you how many rows to count up. For example, the numbers under the first blank tell you to go across 3 and up 1, to the letter I.

What did the student say to the calculator?

$\overline{\text{3,1}}$ $\quad$ $\overline{\text{2,4}}$ $\overline{\text{7,3}}$

$\overline{\text{7,9}}$ $\overline{\text{9,1}}$ $\overline{\text{4,9}}$ $\overline{\text{3,7}}$ $\overline{\text{0,8}}$ $\overline{\text{5,8}}$ $\overline{\text{1,2}}$ $\overline{\text{7,6}}$

$\overline{\text{4,3}}$ $\overline{\text{5,5}}$ $\quad$ $\overline{\text{1,6}}$ $\overline{\text{7,0}}$ $\overline{\text{6,1}}$.

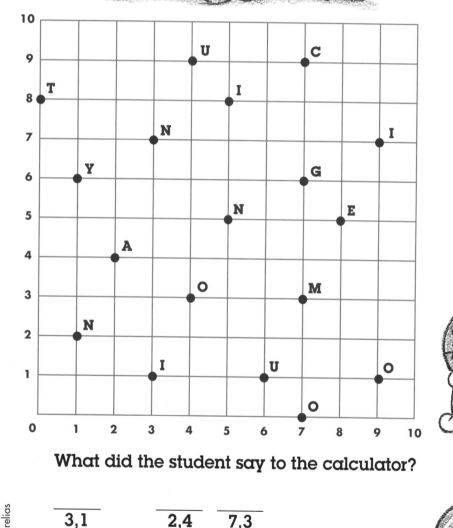
Illustrated by Diana Zourelias

86

Dig Your Starting Holes Deep

from the poem "To James"

by Frank Horne
Art by Lindy Burnett

Dig your starting holes
deep and firm
lurch out of them
into the straightaway
with all the power
that is in you
look straight ahead
to the finish line
think only of the goal
run straight
run high
run hard
save nothing
and finish
with an ecstatic burst
that carries you
hurtling
through the tape
to victory

Wing It!

Each butterfly on these two pages has only one that matches it exactly. Can you find all **12** matching pairs?

89

Crafts

School Supply Holders

By Rebecca Spohn

1. Tape **paper** around a clean, empty **metal can** with no sharp edges.
2. Decorate the can with paper, **markers**, **wiggle eyes**, **chenille sticks**, and **toothpicks**.

Bounce-and-Catch Game

By Marie E. Cecchini

1. On **thin cardboard**, draw a large doughnut shape with a handle attached. Cut it out.
2. Trace the shape once onto another piece of cardboard and twice onto **colored paper**. Cut out the shapes.
3. Cut a large circle from a **mesh produce bag**. Staple the edges to one cardboard doughnut shape.
4. Glue the second cardboard shape to the first, covering the mesh edges.
5. Glue the paper shapes over the cardboard shapes. Use **clothespins** to hold them as the glue dries.
6. Glue **yarn** around the outer edge.

To Play: Hold the net in one hand. With your oth[er] hand, bounce a **table-tennis ball** on the floor. When the ball bounces up, try to catch it in the net. See how many times you can catch it in a row

Photos by Hank Schneider, except page 20 (bottom) by Guy Cali Associates

Personalized Bulletin Board

Katy Efner

Cut two pieces of **corrugated cardboard** the same size. Glue them together to make one thick piece.
Cut one piece of **fabric** 2 inches longer and wider than the cardboard.
Use **masking tape** to tape the fabric around the cardboard.
Cut out letters and shapes from **felt**. Glue them on. Add **rickrack** or **ribbon** as trim.
Tape a **string** hanger to the back.

● ●

Lion Paperweight

Laura Sassi

Find two **rocks** (for the head and body).
Use **tacky craft glue** to glue them together. Let the glue dry.
Paint the lion with a few coats of **acrylic paint**. Let the paint dry.
Glue on **wiggle eyes**. Use a **marker** to draw a mouth and nose.
For the mane, cut short pieces of **yarn** and glue them around the face. For the tail, tie a long piece of yarn around several short pieces, and glue it on.

Magnificent Mosaics

By Linda Gray

1. Using a **pencil**, lightly draw a design on **card stock**.
2. Cut colorful squares from **gift wrap**.
3. Cover part of the design with a thin layer of glue. Place the paper squares on it in an overlapping pattern. Continue until the mosaic is complete.
4. Tape or glue **string** or a **magnet** to the back, or make a greeting card.

91

Pitcher Perfect

This game is heating up. While the teams battle it out, see if you can keep your cool and find at least **20** differences between these pictures.

Which of these players is not at the game today?

Illustrated by Daryll Collins

93

Music Q's

Missing Vowels

SNG TTLS are the words *song titles* with the vowels taken away. Can you figure out the names of these five **SNG TTLS?**

TH STR-SPNGLD BNNR

HPPY BRTHDY T Y

JNGL BLLS

YNK DDL

TK M T T TH BLL GM

Brass or Wind?

Some of these are brass instruments and others are woodwinds. Can you figure out which is which?

TRUMPET
CLARINET
FLUTE
TROMBONE
TUBA
SAXOPHONE
BUGLE
OBOE
PICCOLO
BARITONE HORN

Guess What?

Can you figure out what these two instruments are?

Piano Path

Lina is late for her piano lesson. Can you help her get there on time?

Start →

Finish

Illustrated by Mike Moran

TWIN Guitars

Which two guitars are exactly alike?

A

B

C

D

JUMBLED MUSIC

Unscramble each set of letters to get a type of music.

ZAZJ _ _ _ _

PHI POH _ _ _ _ _ _

REAPO _ _ _ _ _

TRONUCY _ _ _ _ _ _ _

CORK DAN LORL _ _ _ _ _ _ _ _ _ _

Hidden Pictures®
Time for School

flag

heart

bear's head

spatula

lollipop

open book

toothbrush

pennant

trowel

sheep

pencil

drinking straw

wishbone

cupcake

sailboat

slice of cake

ladder

Net Total

The Yellow Jammers and the Blue Dunkers are playing for the school basketball championship. If each player scores the number of points on her jersey, which team will win?

Illustrated by Terry Kovalcik

WHat's FOR LUNCH?

The names of **21** school lunches can fit into this grid. Use the number of letters in each word to figure out where each one belongs. Write in each word and cross it off the list as you go.

When you are finished, copy the letters in the shaded boxes in order from top to bottom and left to right. They will spell the name of the most puzzling lunch of all!

5 letters
Chili
Pizza
Tacos

6 letters
Hot Dog
Nachos

7 letters
Bologna
Lasagna

8 letters
~~Meatloaf~~

9 letters
Chef Salad
Hamburger
Spaghetti

10 letters
Fish Sticks
Sloppy Joes

11 letters
Meatball Sub
Quesadillas

12 letters
Fried Chicken
Peanut Butter

13 letters
Chicken Fillet

14 letters
Chicken Nuggets
Salisbury Steak

17 letters
Macaroni and Cheese

M E A T L O A F

The most puzzling lunch of all is _ _ _ _ _ _ _ _ _ _ _ _ _ _ _ **!**

bird

ruler

mitten

cane

slice of pizza

sailboat

golf club

envelope

magnifying glass

car

scarf

banana

Dot to Dot

Connect the dots from 1 to 24
to see a science fair entry.

Illustration by Dave Klug

For a Change

The Cooper School collecte[d]
money for new books. Th[e]
amounts collected are o[n]
the jars. Can you tell whos[e]
class collected the mo[st]
money and whose collecte[d]
the most coins[?]

Miss Hart

621 pennies
40 nickels
90 dimes
8 quarters

Mrs. Green

200 pennies
20 nickels
100 dimes
32 quarters

Mr. Wiggins

501 pennies
30 nickels
55 dimes
20 quarters

Illustrated by Jim Paillot

PENCIL * PATHS

Which pencil wrote each word?

Illustrated by Jim Steck

Crafts

Desk Organizer

Make your own holder to keep supplies handy and neat.

1. Design your organizer. Choose a variety of tubes and cut sections of differing heights. Decorate with paint and/or colored paper. We painted our tubes and trimmed them with wavy strips of painted paper.

2. Paint the tray and let dry. Then decorate the tray. Finally, glue the tubes to the tray. Hold them in place until the glue sets.

More Ideas

Instead of a plastic-foam tray, use a shoe box lid or trim the bottom 2" from a tissue box. Add MOM or DAD letters for a "special day" gift.

You Will Need:
- cardboard tubes
- colored paper
- paint
- plastic-foam tray
- scissors
- glue
- various items for decoration

"Write" Props

Decorate or play with these oversized and kooky crafts.

To Make the Pencil

Make and decorate a cone for the pencil's point. Ours is about 3" long and made from paper that we decorated with marker and colored pencils. Paint or cover a large tube to look like a pencil. Don't forget the eraser. Insert the wide part of the cone into the other end of the tube and glue or tape.

To Make the Crayon

Choose a color for your crayon. Form a cone for the point from a 2" x 5" rectangle of decorated paper. Cover the opening with a small circle of paper. Decorate the tube. Looking at a real crayon will help with the details. Insert the cone into the tube and secure it with glue or tape. Glue a paper circle over the open end.

You Will Need:
- cardboard tubes
- construction paper
- colored pencils, paint, or markers
- scissors
- glue or tape

More Ideas

To help a preschooler learn colors, make a set of crayons in basic colors.

Make the eraser part of the pencil from a paper cup or piece of tube that is slightly larger than the pencil. Slide the eraser off and store pencils or other surprises inside the tube.

Toadstool Pencil Holder

Is there mush-room for pencils in this holder? There certainly is!

1. To form the cap of the toadstool, carefully turn the open end of the bag so that a few inches of it hang over the sides.

2. Put a rubber band around the section beneath the cap.

3. Paint the toadstool, and let it dry. Put your pencils, pens, and markers in it.

More Ideas

For a puppet-show set, make palm trees by cutting palm fronds from the folded part of the bag.

You Will Need:
- lunch bag
- rubber band
- paints

Autograph Hound

This pooch is perfect for displaying all of your friends' signatures.

1. Cut out a large rectangle from the grocery bag. Fold it accordion-style

2. Open the paper. Use markers to draw a dog across the whole piece of paper.

3. Have your friends sign the card at the end of the school year. Keep it as a memento.

More Ideas

Use the autograph hound as a get-well card from a group of people. Make a similar card using another long animal, such as a giraffe, lizard, otter, or snake.

You Will Need:
- grocery bag
- scissors
- markers

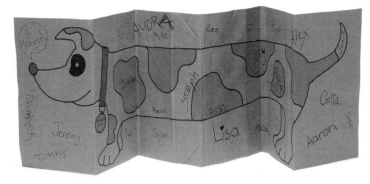

TRY 10

1. Name three words that rhyme with look.

2. What body of water does not touch Florida?
- ○ Atlantic Ocean
- ○ Gulf of Mexico
- ○ Pacific Ocean

3. Circle the symbol that means "recycle."

4. The Spanish word "cantar" means sing.
- ○ True ○ False

5. Name three jellybean flavors

is quiz has 10 questions.
e how many of these you can get right.

6. A new year is "rung in" at hat time?

○ 6 a.m.   ○ noon   ○ midnight

7. Name three animals you might see on an African safari.

8. Spiders lay eggs.
○ True   ○ False

9. Name three egetables that are ot green.

10. Circle the towel with more polka dots.

SQUARE OFF!

Can you figure out what item appears in each picture? Unscramble the name of each.

Answer on page 30

CLEAM

DRAILZ

SONICPRO

RAKEMET

What do they all have in common?

Hidden Pictures
Reading Room

hammer

mug

slice of pie

telescope

crescent moon

magnet

lollipop

pennant

artist's brush

cane

snake

toothbrush

ring

sock

spoon

sailboat

funnel

heart

needle

Fish Fest!

Something's fishy about this puzzle. Actually, everything about it is fishy! Forty kinds of fish are swimming in this grid. Look for them up, down, across, backwards, and diagonally. Can you reel them all in?

Word List

ANCHOVY

ANGELFISH

BARRACUDA

BONEFISH

BURI

CARP

CATFISH

CLOWNFISH

CROAKER

FLOUNDER

GOATFISH

GROUPER

GUITARFISH

GUPPY

HADDOCK

HALIBUT

HERRING

LUNGFISH

MACKEREL

MAHI-MAHI

MARLIN

MINNOW

ORANGE ROUGHY

PERCH

PICKEREL

PIKE

PUFFERFISH

SALMON

SEA BASS

SHARK

SMELT

SOLE

STINGRAY

STURGEON

SWORDFISH

TILAPIA

TROUT

TUNA

WALLEYE

ZANDER

```
P E R C H T U B A R R A C U D A E
L S E L N P U W Q E O C E A N N H
S S C O O O V N D M I N N O W S
H A H W M N V N A G B T A N K I
S B A N L D A F L O U N D E R R
I A L F A Z E S T U R G E O N F
F E I I S G O A T F I S H C E
L S B S W O R D F I S H E B T F
E X U H A D D O C K C S I A U F
G E T C A T F I S H M A F O O U
N I H A M I H A M E M A R L I N P
V A L L E Y E G Y L C S T A P R E I
I P A L I T N T L A K E T G I F C
K O E V S T I N G R A Y I U V I K
J L C H V C R O A K E R U P E S E
O R A N G E R O U G H Y G P R H R
L R M A C K E R E L S A Q Y B G E
K P I K E C H K J H S I F G N U L
```

Touchdown Pass

START

p Ned score a touchdown. Find a path from START to FINISH. If you come to a person, ose a different path.

FINISH

Illustration by Jim Steck

Math Mirth

The Math Club is holding its annual comedy night. Can you guess the answers to these riddles? All the letters you need are in the word list. Each fraction tells you which letters to use.

1. What do you call three feet of trash?

A _ _ _ _   _ _ _ _

First ½ of **AT**
First ½ of **JUNGLE**
Last ½ of **ICKY**
Last ¾ of **CARD**

2. Who invented fractions?

_ _ _ _ _ _ _   _ _   _ _ _

_ _ _ _ _ _ _

Last ¾ of **WHEN**
First ⅔ of **RYE**
First ½ of **THEMES**
Last ⅔ of **SLEIGH**
Middle ⅓ of **MOTHER**

Moon Walk

Twelve men have walked on the moon. Their names can fit in the grid in just one way. Use the number of letters in each person's name as a clue to where it might fit. When you're done, blast to the bottom of the page.

Word List

ALAN BEAN 8
JOHN YOUNG 9
BUZZ ALDRIN 10
DAVID SCOTT 10
PETE CONRAD 10
JAMES IRWIN 10
ALAN SHEPARD 11
CHARLES DUKE 11
EUGENE CERNAN 12
NEIL ARMSTRONG 13
EDGAR MITCHELL 13
HARRISON SCHMITT 15

Bonus Puzzle

Unscramble the six shaded letters to spell the name of the space program that sent these men to the moon.

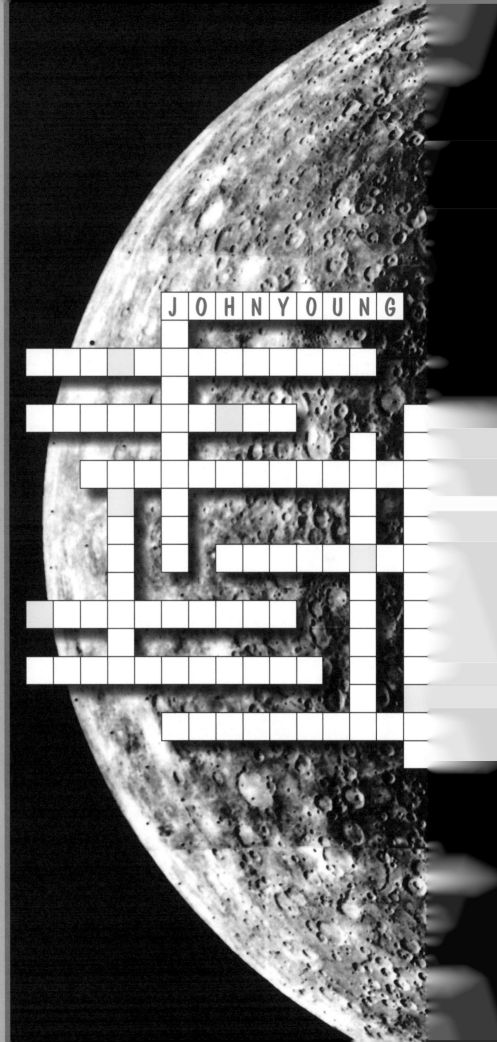

J O H N Y O U N G

Hidden Pictures® Pottery Class

There is more than meets the eye at this pottery studio. Can you find the hidden objects?

Illustrated by Kevin Rechin

bell

spoon

envelope

canoe

flying saucer

baseball cap

ring

fish

comb

horseshoe

kite

ruler

banana

fishhook

heart

muffin

paper clip

hat

spatula

sword

sailboat

baseball bat

carrot

Missing Vowels

Dnsr is the word *dinosaur* with the vowels taken away. Can you figure out the names of these four dnsrs?

TYRNNSRS RX

STGSRS

VLCRPTR

TRCRTPS

Twin Dinos

Which two dinosaurs are exactly alike?

A

B

C

D

A Giant Among Giants

At 60 feet tall, the *Sauroposeidon* is one of the largest dinosaurs ever discovered. This dino is also huge when it comes to words. How many words can you make from the letters in **SAUROPOSEIDON**?

Who Hatched?

What do you think just cracked out of this dinosaur egg? Does it have horns? Scales? A stubby orange tail? Draw your dream dinosaur baby here.

Dig This!

Can you help the paleontologist find her way to the fossil dig?

Start

Finish

DiNO JUMBLE

Unscramble each set of letters to get a word that has to do with dinosaurs.

LISSFO — — — — — —

PETILER — — — — — — —

TEAM ATREE — — — — — — — —

NALPT RETEA — — — — — — — — —

TEXTNIC — — — — — — —

Illustrated by Mike Moran

Pair Squares

Your assignment is to arrange the numbers 1 to 9 inside the colorful cupcake liners. The trick: The numbers in each pair of adjacent cupcake liners must add up to the number in the square pan they touch. Here's a hint to get you started: The number 1 goes in the last cupcake liner on the right.

8   9   12   15

7   11   14   10

Illustrated by Doug Cushman

Shark Sighting!

Keep a good lookout. There are 25 sharks circling in this grid. Search for them up, down, across, backwards, and diagonally. How many can you spot?

Word List

- ANGEL
- BASKING
- BLUE
- BRAMBLE
- BULL
- COOKIE-CUTTER
- COPPER
- GOBLIN
- GREAT WHITE
- HAMMERHEAD
- HORN
- LEMON
- LEOPARD
- MAKO
- NERVOUS
- NURSE
- POCKET
- SAND TIGER
- SAW
- SLEEPER
- SPINY DOGFISH
- THRESHER
- WEASEL
- WHALE
- ZEBRA

```
G N I K S A B N Z E B R A I
O F I N M A K O H T J L U R
G G R E A T W H I T E N U B
C O O K I E C U T T E R P E
D R A P O E L C T J B E R L
T T W M Q J E L E A R P E A
H E E S V T G E K W A P G H
R E A S U T N M C S M O I W
E T S H N O A O O L B C T N
S H E U U A V N P L L U D U
H S L E E P E R I U E S N R
E C S E H O R N E B U N A S
R H S I F G O D Y N I P S E
T A I L H A M M E R H E A D
```

To the T

Claire is meeting her best friend in the cafeteria. She's wearing the exact same T-shirt as Claire. Can you help Claire find her friend?

CLAIRE

Illustrated by Daryll Collins

More Matches

Can you find a pair of exact matches for each of these things, too?

- Lunch bags
- Backpacks
- Books
- Juice boxes
- Posters

123

TRY 10

1. Name three words that rhyme with far.

2. Name two states that begin with the letter A.

3. A rattlesnake's rattle is on its neck.
⚪ True   ⚪ False

5. Circle the v with more flowe

4. The Spanish word "caballo" is this type of animal.
⚪ dog   ⚪ frog   ⚪ horse

6. In which season are pumpkins ready to be picked?

○ fall ○ winter ○ spring

PICK ME

7. Name four animals people keep as pets.

8. Name three things you might put on a hot dog.

9. Potatoes grow underground.

○ True ○ False

10. Circle the largest amount.

Illustrated by Kelly Kennedy

Hidden Pictures®
All Together Now!

pencil

boomerang

flashlight

mitten

candle

hockey stick

muffin

golf club

envelope

sock

butterfly

telephone receiver

funnel

nail

goose

bowl

matchstick

Pebble World

I found a pebble and looked it over.

This could be a whole little world that I held
in my hand.

With its own little trees.
With its own little birds.

I held it and looked as closely as I could,
to see if I could see
any tiny faces smiling back at me.

I couldn't,
but just to be safe,
I placed it carefully back where I had found it.

Natalie J.S. Nida

Illustrated by Gary Phillips

127

WHAT'S THE
BUZZ?

We don't mean to bug you. But we do want you to search for the **35** insects hiding in this grid. Look for them up, down, across, backwards, and diagonally. How many can you spot?

Word List

APHID
BEDBUG
BEETLE
BLOWFLY
BUTTERFLY
CICADA
COCKROACH
CRICKET
DRAGONFLY
EARWIG
FIRE ANT
FIREFLY
FLEA
FRUIT FLY
GNAT
GRASSHOPPER
HONEYBEE
HORNET
HOUSEFLY
KATYDID
LADYBUG
LEAFHOPPER
LOCUST
LOUSE
MANTIS
MAYFLY
MEALYBUG
MIDGE
MOSQUITO
MOTH
SILVERFISH
STINKBUG
TERMITE
WALKING STICK
WEEVIL

```
T E F R U I T F L Y Y L F E R I F
E E B U Z Z T S I L V E R F I S H
R B M N E T M E A L Y B U G O X K
M Y N Y S A L J N C R I C K E T L
I E U U U C O C K R O A C H F G E
T N C L O D D R A G O N F L Y U A
E O F Y L F W O L B R H K P G B F
L H B G U B K N I T S V A H K Y H
E B E D B U G X A W Y U T O W D O
K L Y M B U T T E R F L Y U H A P
M A Y F L Y A V L S R X D S I L P
P D R O N E N V F M X V I E R E E
W A L K I N G S T I C K D F R O R
E W E E V I L E A N V I J L U T S
C A P H E E L G H C M S C Y G P I
H P R C V T D T O F I R E A N T T
I H X W E V O E G D I M D U D V N
R I T E I M O S Q U I T O H N A A
P D B Y P G R A S S H O P P E R M
```

Illustrated by Carolina Farias

Football Fumbles

Are you ready for some football? There are some strange sights at this game. Can you find at least **25** odd, weird, or wacky things in this picture?

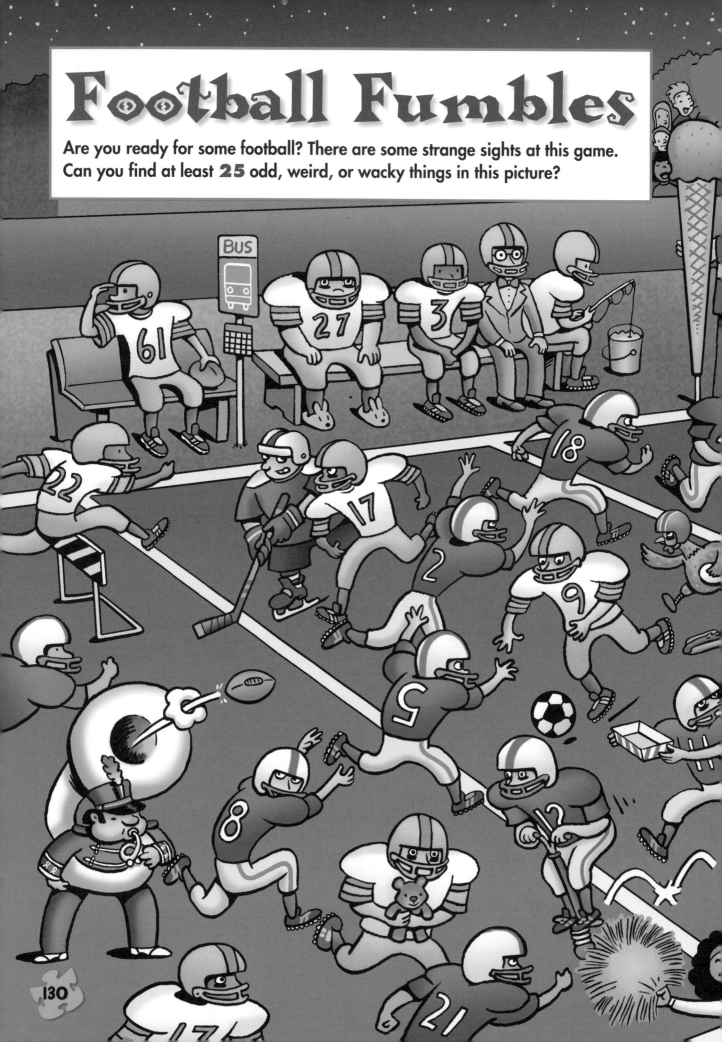

BUS

Illustrated by Tim Haggerty

School Find

The names of 18 school supplies are hidden in the letters. Some words are across. Others are up and down. We found SCISSORS. Can you find the rest?

Word List
ATLAS
CALCULATOR
CHAIR
CHALK
CRAYON
DESK
DICTIONARY
EASEL
ERASER
GLOBE
GLUE
NOTEBOOK
PAPER
PASTE
PENCIL
RULER
SCISSORS
TAPE

```
D I C T I O N A R Y
C H A L K P D E S K
H F L J P A P E R T
A S C I S S O R S A
I Q U V A T L A S P
R U L E R E G L U E
C R A Y O N S W X N
N O T E B O O K Z C
G L O B E A S E L I
Z E R A S E R F J L
```

Illustrated by Jack Desrocher

Answers

5 Catch This!

10–11 Say Cheese!

6–7 Funny Food

What do you call the rear of the lunchroom?
THE BACTERIA

8 Froggie Freedom

9 I Forgot My KROOMHEW

- My baby SISTER tore it up.
- My PENCIL broke.
- A strange ALIEN creature took it on his spaceship.
- The SCHOOL bus splashed mud on it.
- Here it is. I wrote it in INVISIBLE ink.
- A giant TORNADO blew it away.
- A starving CAT ate it.
- My mom was so proud she mailed it to my GRANDMOTHER.
- HOMEWORK? You didn't tell us we had HOMEWORK.

12 Dance Moves

Fiona: Will and tango
Ashley: Owen and cha-cha-cha
Sofia: Sammy and fox-trot
Caryn: Luke and jitterbug

13 By the Numbers

If you add up all the numbers you get 123.
So (123–100) 23 must be the super sub.

14–15 The Run Down

16–17 Try 10

1. Circle the swan.

2. 13

3. Black, brown, blond, and red. Did you think of others?

4. True

5. Collect seashells, swim, boogie board

6. Shirt

7. Circle the plate on the right.

8. Soccer and football

9. False

10. Nap, line, pail, real, alien

133

Answers

19 Back to the Drawing Board

20–21 Zoo Q's

Feed Me!

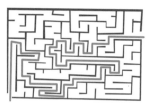

Guess Who?

jaguar – peacock – elephant

Land or Sea?

Land: KOMODO DRAGON, ALPACA, CHINCHILLA, BONGO

Sea: BRITTLESTAR, MANATEE, STINGRAY, BARRACUDA

Jumbled Animals

ZEBRA
CAMEL
PANDA
CHEETAH
POLAR BEAR

Missing Vowels

CHIMPANZEE
BABOON
GORILLA
SPIDER MONKEY
ORANGUTAN

22 Spelling Bee

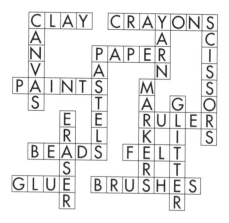

23 Dot to Dot

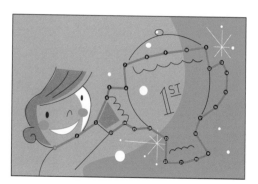

It's a trophy!

24 What's Bugging You?

1. FLIES
2. WORD
3. PETS
4. TYPE
5. HALL
6. SPIN
7 CRAWL
8. WEB SITE
9. WATERSPOUT
10. MULTIPLIES

25 Heading Home

Max: Mr. Jones and Room 25
Robert: Ms. Wilson and Room 200
Jessica: Ms. Russell and Room 100
Willow: Mr. Tripp and Room 125
Mia: Ms. Ames and Room 50

Answers

26–27 Swim Meet

Where do minivans go swimming?
IN A CARPOOL

28–29 5, 4, 3, 2, 1...

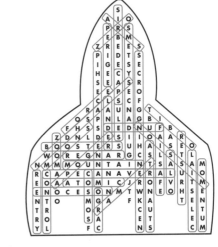

Mission control says, "BLAST OFF!"

32 Making a Mural

33 Tic Tac Row

clouds   stripes   rocket ship   moons

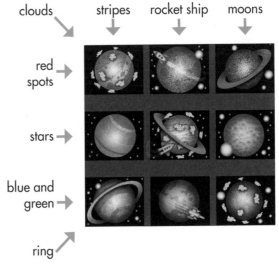

red spots →

stars →

blue and green →

ring ↗

34–35 This Page Has Been Bugged

36–37 Rain Forest Q's

Jungle Journey

Twin Toucans

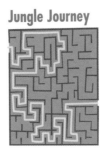

Rain Forest Quiz

1. e   4. c
2. d   5. b
3. a

Creature or Not?

chimpanzee
gibbon
lemur
piranha
anaconda
caiman

Missing Vowels

spider monkey
tree frog
gorilla
jaguar
orangutan

135

Answers

38 What's It Worth?

A = 5 B = 2 C = 6 D = 3 E = 1 F = 4

1. 1 + 2 = 3

2. 2 + 4 = 6

3. 1 × 4 = 4

4. 5 + 5 + 5 + 5 + 5 = 25

5. 6 + 6 + 6 + 6 + 6 + 6 = 36

39 Double Cross

What did the sun say when it was introduced to Earth?
"I'm very pleased to heat you."

42–43 Try 10

1. Soup, ice cream, and cereal. Did you think of others?
2. Triangle
3. Circle the shoe.
4. Indian and Pacific
5. False. New York City is called the Big Apple.
6. Sun
7. Guitar and violin
8. Necklace, scarf, and tie
9. True
10. Circle the monkey on the right.

44–45 Drink Search

46 Be Seated

1. Frank
2. Iris
3. Aiden
4. Grace
5. Carlos
6. Haley
7. Eric
8. Jada
9. Dave
10. Lily
11. Brian
12. Katie

47 School Shopping

136

48–49 Go Team!

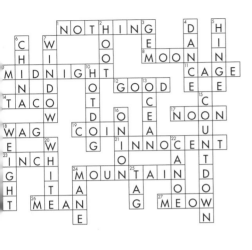

50–51 Color Q's

Color Definitions

- If a company is in the red, it means it made lots of money. FALSE
- Someone who is green with envy is hardly jealous at all. FALSE
- If you are tickled pink, you are extremely happy. TRUE
- A yellow-bellied person is very brave. FALSE
- If something happens once in a blue moon, it almost never happens. TRUE

Shady Quiz

Red
Blue
Green
Purple
Yellow

A Cup-ple of Colors?

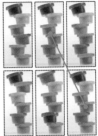

An Animal of Another Color?

Great White Shark
Blue Jay
Black Widow Spider
Red-Eyed Tree Frog
Yellow Jacket
Brown Bear

52–53 A Capital Time

54 An Apple a Day

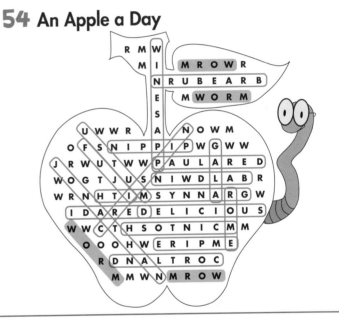

55 Tic Tac Row

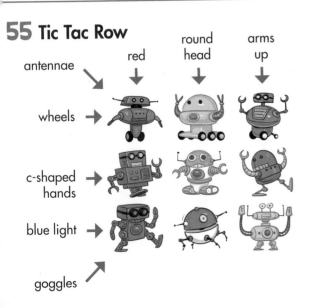

56–57 Lab Labyrinth

Answers

58–59 Try 10

1. Circle the nest.
2. New Mexico, New Jersey, South Carolina, and North Dakota. Did you think of others?
3. Seal, skunk, snake, and squirrel
4. 8
5. True
6. A hybrid
7. False
8. Boot, moon, school
9. Circle the trunk on the left.
10. Ice cream, cottage cheese, pudding, and fruit salad

60 Artists at Work

62–63 Crayon Search

There are nine red and seven blue crayons.

66–67 Space Q's

Look-Alike Landers

Planet X?

Saturn   Jup

Mars   Ear

Space Out!

Here are 21 words we found. You may have found others.

or	oar	use
so	rat	stop
up	rot	tree
cat	sea	true
cup	see	user
ear	toe	sport
eat	top	carpet

Moon Walk

Space Dates

First man on the moon 1969
First man in space 1961
First space walk 1965
First spacecraft landing on Mars........... 1976

68 Bagel Bakers

Andre — 42	Jane — 46
Betty — 88	Larry — 42
Chuck — 84	Mary — 56
Donna — 49	Pablo — 14
Glenn — 98	Sue — 28

Total of all bagels: 547

69 Square Off!

SNAKE   LIZARD

TURTLE   ALLIGATOR

They are all reptiles.

70-71 All Aboard!

72 Field Trip

73 Dot to Dot

It's a seagull!

76 Tic Tac Row

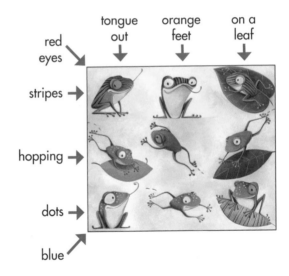

77 Practice Makes Perfect

78-79 Jump on It!

Answers

80 Note Worthy

Dear Reed,

See you at band practice. Bring a ladder so you can reach the high notes! ☺

Your friend,
Melody

82–83 Try 10

1. Circle the sock.
2. Gymnastics
3. Frozen yogurt, berries, juice. Did you think of others?
4. Idaho and Iowa
5. False
6. Red
7. A clown's horn, a tiger's roar, a ringmaster's voice
8. Circle the tennis ball.
9. Pasta
10. True

84–85 Pencil Search

86 Get Coordinated

What did the student say to the calculator? I AM COUNTING ON YOU.

88–89 Wing It!

92–93 Pitcher Perfect

94–95 Music Q's (continued on 141)

Missing Vowels

THE STAR-SPANGLED BANNER
HAPPY BIRTHDAY TO YOU
JINGLE BELLS
YANKEE DOODLE
TAKE ME OUT TO THE BALL GAME

Guess What?

saxophone   drum

Brass or Wind?

Brass: trumpet, trombone, tuba, bugle, baritone horn
Woodwind: clarinet, flute, saxophone, oboe, piccolo

140

94–95 Music Q's (from 140)

Piano Path

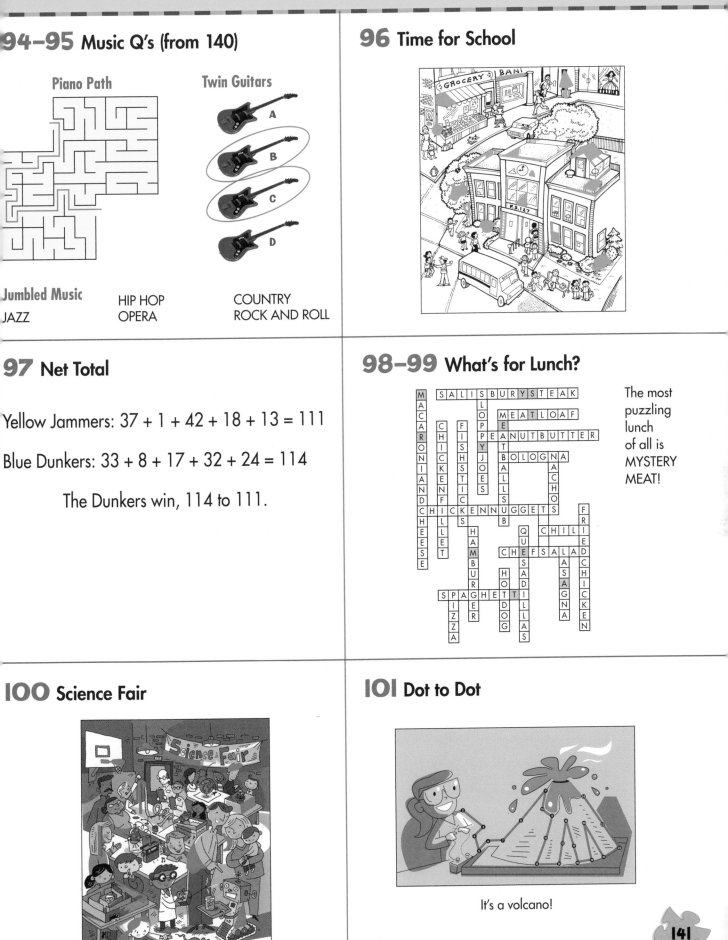

Twin Guitars

A
B
C
D

Jumbled Music

JAZZ

HIP HOP
OPERA

COUNTRY
ROCK AND ROLL

96 Time for School

97 Net Total

Yellow Jammers: 37 + 1 + 42 + 18 + 13 = 111

Blue Dunkers: 33 + 8 + 17 + 32 + 24 = 114

The Dunkers win, 114 to 111.

98–99 What's for Lunch?

The most puzzling lunch of all is MYSTERY MEAT!

100 Science Fair

101 Dot to Dot

It's a volcano!

Answers

102 For a Change

Miss Hart's class collected the most coins
—759.

Mrs. Green's class collected the most money
—$21.00.

103 Pencil Paths

106–107 Try 10

1. Cook, book, and hook. Did you think of others?
2. Pacific Ocean
3. Circle the symbol with three arrows.
4. True
5. Lime, strawberry, and grape
6. Midnight
7. Giraffe, elephant, and rhinoceros
8. True
9. Carrot, eggplant, and butternut squash
10. Circle the towel on the left.

108 Square Off!

CAMEL   LIZARD

SCORPION   MEERKAT

They are all animals that might live in a desert.

109 Reading Room

110–111 Fish Fest!

112–113 Touchdown Pass

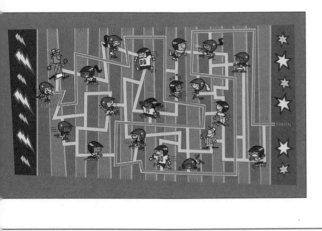

114 Math Mirth

1. A JUNKYARD

2. HENRY THE EIGHTH

115 Moon Walk

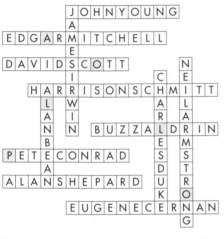

The space program's name was APOLLO.

116–117 Pottery Class

118–119 Dinosaur Q's

Missing Vowels
TYRANNOSAURUS REX
STEGOSAURUS
VELOCIRAPTOR
TRICERATOPS

Dino Jumble
FOSSIL
REPTILE
MEAT EATER
PLANT EATER
EXTINCT

Dig This!

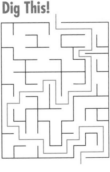

Twin Dinos
A and D match

A Giant Among Giants
Here are some words we made. You may have made others.

ARE	DOOR	NOSE	POISE	PRONE	RUDE
DINE	EARN	OAR	POISED	RIDE	SAID
DINER	IDEA	ODOR	PONIES	RIPE	SIDE
DINOSAUR	NEAR	OPEN	POSE	RIPEN	SOUR
DISEASE	NEED	OUR	POSIE	ROAD	SUPER
DONE	NOD	PASS	POUR	RODE	UNDER
DONOR	NOPE	PASSED	PRIDE	ROPE	USED

120 Pair Squares

Answers

121 Shark Sighting!

```
G N I K S A B N Z E B R A I
O F I N M A K O H T J L U R B
G G R E A T W H I T E N U R
C O O K I E C U T T E R E L
D R A P O E L C T J B E P A H
T T W M Q J E L E A R M P E N
H E E S V T G E K W S A M O U
R A S U T N A E C S M O I R
E S H N O A O O L B C T D S
S H E U U A V N P L L U E N A
H S L E E P E R I U E S D N
E C S E H O R N E B U N A E
R H S I F G O D Y N I P S
T A I L H A M M E R H E A D
```

122–123 To the T

124–125 Try 10

1. Car, star, guitar. Did you think of others?

2. Alabama and Arizona

3. False. It is on the snake's tail.

4. Horse

5. Circle the vase and flowers on the right.

6. Fall

7. Dog, cat, guinea pig, and goldfish

8. Mustard, ketchup, and relish

9. True

10. Circle the quarter and the nickel.

126 All Together Now!

128–129 What's the Buzz?

```
T E F R U I T F L Y Y L F E R I F
E E B U Z Z T S I L V E R F I S H
R B M N E T M E A L Y B U G O X K
M Y E N Y S A L J N C R I C K E T L
I T N C L J C O C K R O A C H F G E
T E O D D R A G O N F L Y U A
E L O F Y L F W O L B R H P G B F H
L H B G U B K N I T S K A T H O O
E B E D B U G A W Y U T H W H P
K L Y M B U T T E R F L Y D A E P
M A Y F L Y A V L S R X D I R O
P D R O N E N V F M X V E R F R T
W A L K I N G S T I C K F S
E W E E V I L E A N V L U T I
A P H E E L C T H M S F I R E A N T M
H X W E V O E G D I M D U D V A
I T E I M O S Q U I T O H N A
P D B Y P G R A S S H O P P E R M
```

132 School Find

```
D I C T I O N A R Y
C H A L K P D E S K
H F L J P A P E R T
A S C I S S O R S A
I Q U V A T L A S P
R U L E R E G L U E
C R A Y O N S W X N
N O T E B O O K Z C
G L O B E A S E L I
Z E R A S E R F J L
```